Zig Ziglar
Little Instruction Book

Inspiration and Wisdom from America's Top Motivator

to life

Mark.

HONOR
B O O K S

Tulsa, Oklahoma

Zig Ziglar's Little Instruction Book
Inspiration and Wisdom from America's Top Motivator
ISBN 1-56292-364-1
Copyright © 1997 by Zig Ziglar
3330 Earhart
Suite 204
Carrollton, TX 75006-5026

Published by Honor Books, Inc.
P.O. Box 55388
Tulsa, Oklahoma 74155

Introduction

Success can be defined in many ways. That is precisely why I have filled this Little Instruction Book with definitions and inspirations that have been most helpful to me on my journey.

I have touched a wide variety of real-life topics, including attitude, praise, self-esteem, determination, time management, personal relationships, and many more . Why? Because I believe you cannot experience true success until it impacts every area of your life. Only then will you truly become the very best that you can be!

Some of the quotes and anecdotes in this book may be familiar to you, but the motivating message behind them is always fresh when the mind and heart are prepared to receive truth. I believe they will provide just the right "pick-me-up" in the midst of your busy day.

I hope you will keep this Little Instruction Book handy as you set your goals, plan your days, and make your way through life. Remember: "In everything you do, put God first, and He will direct you and crown your efforts with success" (Proverbs: 3:6).

Optimists are people who, when they wear out their shoes, just figure they are back on their feet.

I love the way Robert Schuller differentiates between the optimist and the pessimist. An optimist calls a half glass of water "half full," a pessimist "half empty." The reason is simple. The optimist is putting water in the glass. The pessimist is taking water out of the glass. It's almost a universal truth. Anyone taking from society with no real effort to contribute to society is pessimistic because he fears there won't be enough for him. The person who is doing his best and is making a contribution is optimistic and confident because he is personally working on the solution.

When we do more than we are paid to do, eventually we will be paid more for what we do.

As a youngster working in a grocery store in Yazoo City, Mississippi, I knew a young boy who worked in the store across the street.

One day, I asked the manager of my store why Charlie Scott always ran everywhere he went. He replied that Charlie Scott was working for a raise, and he was going to get one. I asked him how he knew. He said that if the man he was working for didn't give him one, that *he* would!

When you turn to God you discover He has been facing you all the time.

Back in the days of sailing ships a young sailor went to sea for the first time. The ship encountered a heavy storm in the North Atlantic. The young sailor was commanded to go aloft and trim the sails. As he started to climb, he made a mistake and looked down. He started to lose his balance. At that moment, an older sailor underneath him shouted, "Look up, son, look up!" The young sailor looked up and regained his balance.

When things seem bad, look to see if you're not facing the wrong direction. When you're looking at the sun, you see no shadows. When the outlook isn't good, try the uplook — it's always good!

You can get everything in life you want, if you help enough other people get what they want.

A man was given a tour of both Heaven and Hell. At first glance, the scene was identical in both places. The inhabitants were seated at a sumptuous banquet table, with forks and knives strapped to their hands. Nonetheless, the inhabitants of hell looked dull and listless and were literally skin and bones. Then the man noticed that the forks and knives had four foot handles which made it impossible to eat.

However with the same forks and knives, the inhabitants of Heaven were well fed and in excellent health. How could such similar circumstances produce such different results? Each person in Heaven was feeding the one across the table from him! By helping one another they helped themselves.

Men of genius are admired. Men of wealth are envied. Men of power are feared, but only men of character are trusted.

— Arthur Friedman

Several years ago I was speaking at a trade school in Tulsa, Oklahoma. Early on, only about one-third of the students were attentively listening. The local television station had gotten word that I was there and sent a camera crew to get some shots. When they walked on the stage behind me, spotlight glaring, 100 percent of the students sat up straight and listened attentively.

In many ways the spotlight is always on all of us as far as our morals, ethics, and responsibilities are concerned. By conducting our lives as if the camera is on, we will be living with integrity, which means we won't have to apologize for, or explain tomorrow, what we did today. This really is a character issue.

God loves you – whether you like it or not!

The Holy Bible tells us that man was created in God's own image. Jesus Christ said, "What I have done, ye can do also and even greater works." He put no superficial qualifications as a requirement to attainment. He didn't leave you out.

Look at it this way. If you are a parent, how do you feel when one of your children says degrading things about himself or herself? How do you think our Heavenly Father feels when we say ugly, deprecating things about ourselves? In reality, we have no right to belittle ourselves.

God would be pleased if you were to take one last look in the mirror before you start your day and say, "God loves you — and so do I."

Make failure your teacher, not your undertaker.

What makes us so afraid of failure? It's worry about what people think. "What will they say?" we ask. We assume that because we've made a mistake, we're failures and therefore forever disgraced. What a ridiculous assumption! How many people are completely successful in every department of life? Not one.

A failure means you've put forth some effort. That's good. Failure gives you an opportunity to learn a better way to do it. That's positive. A failure teaches you something and adds to your experience. That's very helpful. Failure is an event, never a person; an attitude, not an outcome; a temporary inconvenience; a stepping-stone. Our response to it determines just how helpful it can be.

Where you start is not as important as where you finish.

A study of three hundred world-class leaders, including Franklin D. Roosevelt, Sir Winston Churchill, Helen Keller, Mother Teresa, Dr. Albert Schweitzer, and Martin Luther King, Jr., revealed that 25 percent of them had serious physical disabilities and an additional 50 percent had been abused as children or were raised in poverty. These leaders *responded* instead of *reacted* to what happened to them.

Neil Rudenstien's father was a prison guard and his mother a part-time waitress. Today, Dr. Neil Rudenstien is president of Harvard University. He says he learned very early in life that there is a direct correlation between performance and reward.

Rudenstien and the three hundred world-class leaders personally learned that it's not where you start — it's where you finish that counts.

These ten little
two-letter words
— *If it is to be it is up to me*
— are absolutely valid.
The solution is to do it now.

I believe *fear* (which is faith in reverse) is a major reason for not using our talents. Many people don't understand that failure is an event and not a person, so they decide to play it safe and not do anything at all. Then they will not have failed because they never tried.

Some of the saddest words you'll ever hear are "what might have been." Speaker Vicki Hitzges puts it in a unique and different way when she asks, "Will you look back on life and say, 'I wish I had' or 'I'm glad I did?' " Following these success principles will make it possible for you to look back one day and say, "I'm glad I did." You do have a choice.

Love...does not hold grudges and will hardly even notice when others do it wrong.

— 1 Corinthians 13:5

The True Love Daily Checklist

1. Did I speak words of love to my mate today?

2. Was I patient with my mate today?

3. Was I kind to my mate today?

4. Was I jealous or envious of my mate today?

5. Was I selfish with or rude to my mate today?

6. Did I demand my own way with my mate today?

7. Did I hold on to grudges against my mate today?

8. Was I loyal to my mate today?

9. Did I use my strengths for my mate today?

Do you know a hard-working man? He shall be successful and stand before kings!

— Proverbs 22:29

The profile of a wealthy person is this: hard work, perseverance, and most of all, self-discipline. The average wealthy person has lived all his adult life in the same town. He's been married once and is still married. He lives in a middle-class neighborhood next to people with a fraction of his wealth. He's a compulsive saver and investor, and he's made his money on his own. Eighty percent of America's millionaires are first-generation rich. (Doesn't sound like opportunity is dead to me.)

Put all your excuses aside and remember this: *You* are capable.

Inject people with hope.

almost failed as a salesman. I had struggled for 2-1/2 years. I was on a losing streak, but I never saw myself as a loser. I still had the fear of rejection. I didn't understand that prospects weren't rejecting me, they were only rejecting the offer I was making them.

If it wasn't for some words of encouragement from my company president, P.C. Merrell, I would have probably found another job. Merrell said, "Ziglar, you have real ability, you're champion caliber, I'm looking at you as a future officer of this company." Those words inspired me to become the number two salesman in a company of 7,000 in one year.

If a child lives with praise, he learns to appreciate.

— Dorothy Nolte

Children Live What They Learn
by Dorothy Law Nolte

If a child lives with criticism,
He learns to condemn.
If a child lives with hostility,
He learns violence.
If a child lives with ridicule,
He learns to be shy.
If a child lives with shame,
He learns to feel guilty.
If a child lives with encouragement,
He learns confidence.

If a child lives with praise,
He learns to appreciate.
If a child lives with fairness,
He learns justice.
If a child lives with security,
He learns faith.
If a child lives with approval,
He learns to like himself.
If a child lives with acceptance
and friendship,
He learns to love the world.

The difference between a big shot and a little shot is that a big shot's just a little shot that kept on shooting.

While being questioned by a young reporter about an invention he had been working on for a long time, Thomas Edison revealed one of the secrets of his greatness. The young reporter asked, "Mr. Edison, how does it feel to have failed 10,000 times in your present venture?" Edison replied, "Young man, I will give you a thought that should benefit you in the future. I have not failed anything 10,000 times. I have successfully found 10,000 ways that will not work."

Edison estimated that he actually performed over 14,000 experiments in the process of inventing and perfecting the incandescent light. He successfully found a lot of ways that wouldn't work, but he kept at it until he found one way that would!

Hard work means prosperity; only a fool idles away his time.

— Proverbs 12:11

I can't believe that failure is caused by lack of opportunity, because America offers many unique opportunities. For example, several years ago a wealthy prisoner was released from the Federal Prison in Atlanta, Georgia. He had a built-in Loser's Limp. Nevertheless, he accumulated a small fortune by operating a tailor shop in prison. After his big mistake had landed him in prison, he was determined not to make a bigger one by "serving time." He made time serve him.

In a real sense you have the same choice. Choose to make time your servant, not your master.

Failure is the line of least persistence.

ZIG ZIGLAR'S Little Instruction Book

There was once a young man who was involved in an oil venture and ran out of money, so he sold his interest to his partners who stuck with it. After much time and effort, they got their break and hit a gusher. The company later became Cities Service, and we know it today as CITGO. The young man who withdrew, later got involved in the clothing business and fared even worse than he had in the oil business. As a matter of fact, he went broke. Still, he wasn't discouraged. Later on he got into politics.

Historians have many kind things to say about Harry S. Truman, the two-time failure who kept getting back up until he became President of the United States.

You are not a failure until you quit trying.

35

It is not what happens to you that determines how far you go in life; it is what you do with what happens to you.

One of the most remarkable men I've ever known is Charlie Wedemeyer from Los Gatos, California. Charlie coached the Los Gatos high school football team to the only state championship they've ever won.

The amazing thing is that the only parts of his body he can move are his eyes and mouth. Charlie Wedemeyer suffers from Lou Gehrig's disease. Charlie's example of commitment and courage while maintaining his upbeat attitude toward life is an inspiration to literally millions of people.

When you see Charlie and talk with him, you realize that his very life is an inspiration, and it makes you want to do more with what you have. Wherever he goes, people from all walks of life agree that Charlie Wedemeyer's life makes a profound statement. Does yours?

You will make a lousy anybody else, but you are the best "you" in existence. You are the only one who can use your ability. It is an awesome responsibility.

I've become completely convinced over the years that the overwhelming majority of people in our great country have a picture of themselves that is so narrow and shallow that it bears little or no resemblance to who they are or what they can do.

Far too many people have no idea of what they can do because all they have been told is what they can't do. Unfortunately, too many people see how success and the good life would be available for everybody else, but they protest, "For me? No way!"

Just having ability and intelligence is not the key — it's recognizing that ability, confessing it, appreciating it, developing it, and then using it.

The parent who truly has a good self-image understands that real love demands they do what is best for the child.

There are going to be many instances as you raise your kids when it would be easier and less hassle to simply give in to their demands. On many occasions, it will be easier to plop the kids in front of the television set or let them eat the junk food.

Later it will be easier to allow them to stay up until ten instead of having to explain why they need to be in bed by nine. Still later it will be easier to let them start dating early and stay out too late so they can be "like all the other kids." However, real love demands you do what is best for your children and not necessarily what they want you to do.

You love your kids. Decide today to keep their best in mind at all times.

For a child, love is spelled T-I-M-E.

A young man was to be sentenced to the penitentiary. The judge had known him from childhood and was well acquainted with his father, a famous legal scholar. "Do you remember your father?" asked the magistrate. "I remember him well, your honor," came the reply. Then the judge asked, "As you are about to be sentenced and as you think of your wonderful dad, what do you remember most clearly about him?"

There was a pause. Then the judge received an unexpected answer. "I remember when I went to him for advice, he looked at me from the book he was writing and said, 'Run along, boy; I'm busy!' Your honor, you remember him as a great lawyer. I remember him as a lost friend."

Our children need our time more than anything else; not just quality, but quantity.

The real opportunity for success lies within the person and not in the job; you can best get to the top by getting to the bottom of things.

I wish it were possible for me to introduce to you the scores of very talented people I have met who are generally just one step ahead of the bill collector and often just two steps ahead of the law. They are always looking for a "deal" and the "fast buck." They never build very much or very high, because they have no foundation to build on. Others with the right foundation end up living in the basement or building a chicken shack on that foundation. They don't take all the steps to use the talent they have to get the richer life.

Success and happiness are not matters of chance, but choice. You literally choose what you want in life.

I've got to say no to the good so I can say yes to the best.

About every five or six years, at the beginning of the year, I engage in a little process that is meaningful to me. The last time I did this I let my imagination dwell on anything and everything I wanted to do during the new year.

I tried to evaluate how much time would be required each week to do all of the things I wrote down, and counting 7 hours of sleep per night, it came to a total of over 300 hours a week. Since there are only 168 hours in the week, I realized something very significant: I had to eliminate much of the good so I could choose the best. That's what I'm encouraging you to do.

We deplete nature's natural resources by using them up. We deplete man's natural resources by failing to use them.

For a long time I thought the most tragic thing that could happen to man would be to discover an oil well on his property as he lay on his deathbed. Now I know that it is infinitely worse to never discover the vastly greater wealth that lies within the individual. As a good friend says, "A dime and a $20 gold piece have the same value if they are corroding at the bottom of the ocean." The difference in value is manifested only when you lift those coins up and use them as they were intended to be used.

Your value becomes real and marketable when you learn to reach within yourself and utilize the enormous potential that is there.

It seems universally true that people who have direction in their lives go farther and faster and get more done in all areas of their lives.

David G. Jensen, from the UCLA School of Medicine, surveyed the people who attend public seminars I conduct. He divided them into two groups: Those who set goals and developed a plan of action to reach them, and those who took no specific action to set their goals.

The goal setters earned an average of twice as much per month as the nonaction group. Not surprisingly, the action group tended to be more enthusiastic, more satisfied with life and work, happier in marriage, and their overall health was better.

As Mr. Jensen stated, "These results also confirm the academic literature on goals that, over the past 20 years, have shown unequivocally that those who set goals perform better in a variety of tasks." Setting goals works!

When you break goals into increments and start controlling your time, things begin to happen.

Frequently, the difference between the great and the "near" great is the realization that if you expect to make it big, you must work toward your objectives every day. The weight lifter knows that if he is going to accomplish a big objective, he must strengthen and expand his muscles every day. The parents who would raise a disciplined, loving child know that character and faith are built by daily injections of teaching-by-example.

Daily objectives are the best indicators of character. This is where dedication, discipline and determination enter the picture. Here we take the glamour of the big, long-range goal and get right down to the nitty-gritty of foundation building that will help make certain that your dream becomes your destiny.

How do you eat an elephant? Yes, one bite at a time!

By the mile it's a trial, but by the inch it's a cinch.

My first book, *See You at the Top,* has 384 pages. After completing the research, I wrote the book in ten months. That boils down to writing an average of 1.26 pages per day.

You raise positive kids in a negative world by giving daily injections of time, love, and attention to your children. You build a beautiful marriage by the daily application of kindness, consideration, respect, faithfulness, thoughtfulness, and attentiveness to your mate. You build a successful career, regardless of your field of endeavor, by the dozens of little things you do on and off the job.

You reach those significant goals by breaking them into small segments.

Some people find fault like there was a reward for it.

For years I have been encouraging individuals who are unhappy to change from being faultfinders to being good-finders. I suggest they make a list of all the things they like, admire, or appreciate about their job, mate, or city. Then I encourage them to enthusiastically verbalize those things in front of a mirror each morning and evening.

Recently, in a presentation in Dallas, I suggested that audience members list things they liked about their jobs. Two weeks later a woman told me she followed through on my suggestion, and in less than a week her supervisor was complimenting her on her new attitude and the improvement in her performance.

The more you recognize and express gratitude for the things you have, the more things you will have to express gratitude for.

Direction literally creates time.

Perhaps the greatest advantage of having a goals program is the freedom that goes with having direction in your life. When your goals are clearly defined and intelligently set, you have, in essence, taken a major step toward programming your left brain. That frees our right brain to be its creative best.

The best analogy I can give you is the superbly conditioned and gifted athlete who is so disciplined and committed to the fundamentals of the game that he or she is free to be at their creative best. When unique situations arise where the athlete must improvise to make the big play, coaches of gifted athletes will typically say, "You can't coach that."

Direction creates time and frees the brain to think creatively and innovatively. Where are you going today?

When a job is loved, work makes life sweet, purposeful, and fruitful.

Several years ago, when I was on a speaking tour of Australia, I met a young man named John Nevin who had the right mental attitude. He was in love with life, his family, and with his job. He not only had a "job" selling the World Book Encyclopedia, but the job had him, which meant that his progress was fast and inevitable. He moved from being a "part timer" just fourteen years ago to Managing Director of Field Enterprises for Australia. Then, John become the second non-American to be elected to the board of Field Enterprises, USA. He is financially secure and grateful for the fact that he is living and working in a country that believes in the free enterprise system.

Sometimes, the difference between loving your job and hating your job is all in your attitude.

Children pay more attention to what you do than what you say.

— Mamma Ziglar

A solid foundation for children involves a solid moral base. Parents who teach their children honesty, but fail to practice it themselves create real problems.

For example, suppose parents repeatedly tell their children to be truthful, but when the telephone rings, they call out to the child who's answering it, "Tell them I'm not home." The message to the child is clear. If children are taught to lie *for* parents, they are taught to lie *to* parents.

As another example, suppose parents lecture their children on the importance of obeying the law, yet install a radar detector in the car to avoid being stopped for speeding. The message again is clear. If you're going to break the law, don't get caught.

Good values are easier caught than taught.

The Success Family has work as the father and integrity as the mother.

Work is the foundation of all business, the source of all prosperity and the parent of genius.

Work can do more to advance youth than his own parents, be they ever so wealthy.

It is represented in the humblest savings and has laid the foundation of every fortune.

It is the salt that gives life its savor but it must be loved before it can bestow its greatest blessing and achieve its greatest ends.

When loved, work makes life sweet, purposeful, and fruitful.

— Anonymous

It is far more important to be
the right kind of person
than it is to marry
the right kind of person.

Once while traveling, I noticed the fellow next to me had his wedding band on the index finger of his right hand. I commented, "Friend, you've got your wedding band on the wrong finger." He responded, "Yeah, I married the wrong woman."

Many people have wrong ideas about marriage. You may very well have married the wrong person. However, if you treat the wrong person like the right person, you could end up having married the right person after all. On the other hand, if you marry the right person and treat them wrong, you certainly will end up with the wrong person.

In short, whether you married the right or wrong person is primarily up to *you*.

You are the way you are because that's the way you want to be. If you really wanted to be any different, you would be in the process of changing right now.

— Fred Smith

The difference between me and many others who want to be speakers is that I never let go of my dream or the willingness to work toward achieving it. Most people who fail in their dream fail not from lack of ability, but from lack of commitment. Commitment produces consistent, enthusiastic effort that inevitably produces greater and greater rewards.

You develop the qualities of success and bring them to full maturity in much the same way I brought my speaking career to a full-time occupation. I made the decision to "do."

Unless you decide to "do" whatever it takes to acquire the qualities necessary for success, you might end up never realizing what you could have been.

The best thing a parent can do for a child is to love his or her spouse.

This reality was brought home to me when my son was about fifteen years old. We were taking a walk and I asked him, "Son, if anyone should ask you what you liked best about your dad, what would you say?"

He said, "I'd say that the thing I like best about my dad is that he loves my mom." Naturally I asked, "Son, why would you say that?" He replied, "I know because you love Mom you're going to treat her right, and as long as you treat her right, we will always be a family, because I know how much Mom loves you. That means, Dad, that I will never have to choose between you and Mom."

"Husbands, show the same kind of love to your wives as Christ showed to the Church." (Ephesians 5:25.)

Caring is more than compromise and more than mutual agreement not to hurt each other. It is a tacit agreement to help each other.

— Anonymous

When I was in the cookware business, I one day found that I had made more appointments than I could keep. I asked my assistant, Gerry Arrowood, who did all the work while I did all the talking, to deliver six sets of cookware for me. Since she wasn't accustomed to talking to customers, she did not want to do it, but finally said she would.

The next night I got one of the most exciting phone calls I've ever received. Gerry said, "I don't ever remember having this much fun or feeling so good about myself. I'll be glad to do this for you anytime you want me to!" Her picture [of herself] had just undergone a dramatic change.

By helping others you help yourself.

Don't wait until you feel like taking a positive action. Take the action and then you will feel like doing it.

Remember Gerry? After taking that first step, she became highly motivated, and her self-image improved dramatically. Her confidence started to soar and she became more assertive. She started setting bigger goals; her optimism rose; she became more positive. The results speak for themselves.

Let me point out that Gerry started with only courage, compassion, pride, and humility; she was conscientious, absolutely dependable, and a very hard worker. She developed the other qualities of successful people as a direct result of using what she already had.

That's a tremendous lesson for you to learn about motivation! Don't miss a major, major point. The motivation came after she took action.

A sincere compliment is one of the most effective teaching and motivational methods in existence.

As a young salesman, I read a story that made a lasting impression. A woman who had once had a tremendous career as a singer had been so discouraged by the criticism of her teacher she eventually quit singing altogether.

Her talent lay dormant until an exuberant salesman began courting her. On occasion, when she would hum a little tune or a melody would burst forth, he would marvel at the beauty of her voice. "Sing some more, Honey. You have the most beautiful voice in all the world," he would say. He showered her with praise. Not too surprisingly, her confidence returned and she began to receive invitations to sing again. She eventually married the "good-finder" and went on to a successful career.

A sincere compliment can produce sensational results.

You cannot receive a sincere compliment without feeling better...and just as important, you cannot give a sincere compliment without feeling better yourself!

Part of our hesitancy in sharing compliments comes from the fear of being misunderstood. If a man greets an attractive lady at a business or social occasion with, "That's a beautiful dress," she might wonder about his motive. If you compliment a male acquaintance with, "That's a great looking watch you have on," he might well think you're trying to set him up for a future favor or even a small loan. Even though both compliments would be sincere, we often don't share them because of the fear of being misunderstood. This results in two people losing.

A sincere compliment makes both the giver and the receiver feel good. Sharing the compliment results in a double win!
Don't be afraid — go for it!

Efficiency is doing things right. Effectiveness is doing the right things.

— Thomas K. Connellan

The proper utilization of our time and resources, involves some truths which are so simple and basic that many people miss them completely. First, we need to understand that there is no point in doing well that which you should not be doing at all. When you take on a task, you should ask yourself if this is something you should be doing, or is it something someone else should be doing.

According to research, 10-15 percent of the tasks managers are personally handling should be delegated and 10-15 percent should be eliminated. What tasks can you eliminate today? What tasks can you delegate to someone else? Focus on effective use of time rather than just efficient use of time.

LOST — Somewhere between sunrise and sunset — one golden hour encrusted with sixty silver minutes, each studded with sixty diamond seconds. No reward is offered. They are lost and gone forever.

— Anonymous

Everyone gets twenty-four hours a day — sixty minutes for every hour and sixty seconds for every minute. No one can get more; no one can get less. You can't build a bigger time pipeline and say, "I want more." No one can live more than one second at a time. In this sense, everyone is truly equal. Now this one fact alone makes time the most precious of all commodities. This factor forces us to an inescapable conclusion: We've got to make our time work for us — it's the most perishable and nonnegotiable possession we have. We have to get production out of every second.

Time is the only commodity we deal with which cannot be counterfeited, stolen, or placed in inventory. Remember, time is irreplaceable.

What you do off the job plays a major role in how far you go on the job. How many good books do you read each year? How often do you attend workshops? Who do you spend most of your time with?

A classic example of someone who hasn't finished her education is Laurie Magers, my administrative assistant. She came to work with less than a high-school education, but she clearly understood that she could continue her education. She's an avid reader and a good student of vocabulary. She attends lectures and seminars on a regular basis, and has for many years.

When we conducted a comprehensive evaluation for the key people in our company, Laurie scored slightly higher than the master's level of education average. To me, that says a great deal. Because Laurie continued her education on and off the job, she has not only job security at our company, but employment security, should something happen to our company.

Work to have employment security instead of just job security.

As the earth revolves around the sun, so should our lives also revolve around the Son.

On July 4, 1972, I declared my complete *dependence* on Jesus Christ, an event which completely changed my life. However, even though I claim July 4th as my "born again" day, I'm not certain that it actually happened that day. For me, there was no clanging of bells or flashing of lights. But, there was a warm, solid feeling of complete confidence that God saw my heart, heard my confession of sin, and welcomed me into His Kingdom. It's important that you understand this because many people never have an earth-shattering moment of ecstasy. If you don't, or didn't, don't be concerned. You are not saved by a feeling, but by trusting God and accepting Jesus Christ as your Savior.

Have you celebrated your "Dependence Day"?

You can no more do God's work without God than you could have sunshine without the sun.

Not long after I turned my life over to the Lord, a man I met noticed my "fish and seven" pin. He said, "I know what the fish means, but what does the 'seven' mean?" I explained that there are seven days in the week and they all belong to the Lord. I explained that I had recently turned my life entirely over to the Lord and that it had made a dramatic difference.

He said, "I know exactly what you mean." He went on to say that for over fifteen years he had served as a choir director in one of the local churches but had not known Jesus Christ personally until recently.

Many people profess Christ, but do not possess Him.

The price of success is much lower than the price of failure.

This little story Charles Getts tells in *Guideposts* emphasizes the attitude of "enjoying" the price.

In old age, Pierre Auguste Renoir, the great French painter, suffered from arthritis, which twisted and cramped his hand. Henri Matisse, his artist friend, watched sadly while Renoir, grasping a brush with only his fingertips, continued to paint, even though each movement caused stabbing pain.

One day, Matisse asked Renoir why he persisted in painting at the expense of such torture.

Renoir replied, "The pain passes, but the beauty remains."

Man was designed for accomplishment, engineered for success, and endowed with the seeds of greatness.

From my vantage point, the truly "beautiful people" come from every walk of life. I've seen people who have succeeded sometimes because of, and many times in spite of, almost unbelievable handicaps. They refused to accept a Loser's Limp and became quite successful, happy, and well-adjusted individuals in the process. Their stories are the most beautiful stories we can encounter.

Without exception, these people believe the quote on the opposite page. When you adopt this belief you will discover that there will be no need to blame anyone for any problem. In short, you will be on your way because you will have discovered that you can always find a capable, helping hand at the end of your own sleeve.

There is little you can learn from doing nothing.

Easily, the most puzzling incident in the sport's world occurs in baseball when a batter steps up to the plate and lets the pitcher throw three strikes without taking a single cut at the ball. He has three opportunities and he never moves the bat from his shoulder. He "saw" himself striking out. He left his bat on his shoulder hoping for a "walk" — a free ride to first base.

Even more disappointing is to see a person in the ball game of life step up to the plate, and never really take a cut at the ball. He is the biggest failure of all because he doesn't try.

If you try,m and lose, you can learn from losing — which greatly reduces the loss!

Take what you have and use it, and your talent will be increased.

Surely you remember the story of the talents in the Bible. One man had one, another had two, still another had five. When their lord returned from his travels he asked them what they had done with the talents. The man with five invested his and had five more. The man with two multiplied his. The man who was given one went and buried it.

The lord said, "Thou wicked and slothful servant." And He took the one talent and gave it to the one who had ten. Since that time, the cry-babies of the world have been saying, "The rich get richer and the poor get poorer." The Bible says, "To him who hath, the more shall be given."

We must not bury our talents, but invest them, spend them, pour them out. Then, we will have even more.

Life is an echo. What you send out — comes back.

Once a little boy in a fit of anger shouted to his mother that he hated her. Fearing punishment, he ran out of the house to the hillside and shouted into the valley, "I hate you, I hate you, I hate you." The valley echoed back, "I hate you, I hate you, I hate you." Startled, the boy ran back and told his mother there was a little boy in the valley saying he hated him. His mother told him to return and shout, "I love you, I love you." The little boy did and this time he discovered there was a nice little boy in the valley saying, "I love you, I love you."

Remember, what you say comes back to you!

The way you see yourself today will affect your performance today.

Right pictures and wrong pictures can be painted with one sentence. The person who says, "I hope I don't forget," or "Don't let me forget," has just given himself the wrong instructions. It's far better for him to say, "I'm going to remember that I placed the keys in my top desk drawer."

The list can be endless. I encourage you to take a notepad and each time you catch yourself saying something that paints a negative picture, write down what you've just said and then rephrase it to paint a positive picture.

The most influential person who will talk to you all day is you, so you should be very careful about what you say to you!

A lot of people have gone further than they thought they could because someone else thought they could.

ZIG ZIGLAR'S Little Instruction Book

A New York businessman dropped a dollar into the cup of a man selling pencils and stepped aboard the subway train. Then he stepped back off the train, and took several pencils from the cup. He explained he had neglected to pick up his pencils. "After all," he said, "you are a businessman just like myself. You have merchandise to sell and it's fairly priced."

A few months later, a neatly-dressed salesman stepped up to the man and introduced himself. "You probably don't remember me but I will never forget you. You are the man who gave me back my self-respect. I was a 'beggar' selling pencils until you came along and told me I was a businessman."

You never know what one word of encouragement can do for someone today. Don't hesitate to give it.

Men and women are limited not by the place of their birth, not by the color of their skin, but by the size of their hope.

— John Johnson

John Johnson was raised in Arkansas City, Arkansas, the geographical center of the world. You can start there and go anywhere in the world you want to go — and never go more than twelve thousand miles. Mr. Johnson went less than two thousand miles from the tin-roofed shotgun house where he was born, but far enough to live on Chicago's Gold Coast and next door to Bob Hope in Palm Springs, California. He has been listed as one of the four hundred wealthiest men in America.

You, too, are fortunate because regardless of where you live you are in the geographical center of the world. You can go from where you are to anywhere you want to go.

Important: Until you commit your goals to paper you have intentions that are seeds without soil.

— Anonymous

Goal setting is demanding, which is one of the reasons only 3 percent of us have a goals program. This is also one reason the rewards for those who have a program are so great.

The thought of investing the time necessary might be overwhelming, and you might feel you simply don't have the time right now.

If you don't have time to invest in establishing a goals program, is it possible that you don't have time because you don't have a goals program? In all probability, lack of time always has been and always will be the problem.

Make a commitment to establish a goals program now and you will have more time in the future to do what you need to do and want to do.

You get the best out of others when you give the best of yourself.

— Harvey Firestone

When General Schwarzkopf was interviewed by Barbara Walters, she asked him for his definition of leadership. He reflected for a moment and said, "It's competence. More important, it's character. It's taking action. It's doing the right [ethical] thing." These four qualities are critical for success in the business world.

Later Barbara asked him what he wanted on his tombstone. With just the hint of a tear in his eye, he said, "I want it to say, 'He loved his family and he loved his troops — and they loved him.'"

Having the ability to walk in the shoes of another is of paramount importance. When you truly know how the other person feels, you can communicate with him or her more easily and lead more effectively.

Money will buy all kinds of things for my family, but it won't buy their love.

I confess that I was once like the young man who equated security with money and money with success. I was able to help him see where his perspective was off because life had taught me that true contentment and total success come from the things money can't buy. Don't misunderstand. I like the things money can buy, and I'll bet you do, too. I like nice clothes, a beautiful residence, big, comfortable cars, and so on. However, I love the things money won't buy. It will buy me a house, but not a home; a bed, but not a good night's sleep; pleasure, but not happiness; a good time, but not peace of mind; and a companion, but not a friend.

Success is not equal to money. True success involves every area of your life.

Kids go where there's excitement. They stay where there's love.

I challenge you, next time the phone rings and one of your children is near, to answer it with an enthusiastic, "Good morning, this is Molly's proud mom!" or "Good morning, this is Paul's proud poppa!" You'll be amazed at what will happen the first few times you do it. Your fourteen-year-old may shrug his shoulders and say, "Aw, Dad!" but I can guarantee you, the next time the phone rings, he will wait for you to answer it in the hopes you'll answer it in the same way. The reason is simple: You are stroking him by verbalizing your love for him and his importance to you. At the same time you're visibly demonstrating that enthusiasm is important.

One definition of insanity is to believe that you can keep on doing what you've been doing and get different results.

Let me ask you a couple of questions, which are primarily designed to give you comfort and encouragement: Is there a possibility that you're not as far along in life as you would like to be? Is it because you don't have the ability or it is far more likely that you have everything it takes, but you have been following the wrong plan of action for your life?

Now you're faced with a choice. You can choose to keep on doing (following the same blueprint) what you've been doing, which means you'll keep on getting what you've been getting, or you can choose to accept that you do have what it takes (and you do), but you've been following the wrong blueprint.

When you choose to be pleasant and positive in the way you treat others, you have also chosen, in most cases, how you are going to be treated by others.

One day my son, Tom, and I were headed home, after playing in a golf tournament. We walked to the gate to catch our flight, and there were roughly 1,121 irate passengers waiting to get their boarding passes.

As my son and I stepped up, I enthusiastically greeted the ticket agent, "Good morning. How ya doin'?"

The young man looked at me and replied, "Compared to whom?"

"Compared to the individual who doesn't have a job, who doesn't have warm clothes to wear. How ya doin'?" He replied, "I'm doing much better — thank you very much for reminding me."

We were bumped to first class and the ticket agent greeted the remaining passengers with enthusiasm and courtesy.

Motivation fuels that attitude that builds the confidence necessary to sustain the persistence.

One football team is dominating another when a big break suddenly occurs for the losing team and every athlete on the team instantly feels a sense of excitement, fueled by hope that turns to belief that they can — and will — win the game. They feel victory, and that feeling is reinforced by the look in the eyes of the opposing players.

Life is that way. When we sense that something positive is going to happen, we're energized. When we fear we're going to lose, we are de-energized. That's why motivation is important.

That's the reason a person who wants to maximize life will deliberately schedule regular motivational input just as surely as he will schedule putting food into his stomach.

Check the records. There has never been an undisciplined person who was a champion. Regardless of the field of endeavor, you'll find this to be true.

Discipline, according to the dictionary, means "to instruct or educate, to inform the mind, to prepare by instructing in correct principles and habits; to advance and prepare by instruction." Author Sybil Stanton says true discipline isn't on your back, needling you with imperatives. It is at your side, nudging you with incentives. These are better pictures because they build hope for the future.

The great violinist Isaac Stern was asked, "Is talent born?" He responded yes, talent is born, but musicians are made. It takes an incredible amount of discipline, hard work, and talent to become a great musician.

No matter how great the talent or the field of endeavor, unless the individual is personally disciplined much of the potential will remain just that — potential.

You're not old until you have lost all of your marvels.

— Anonymous

When Bismarck was chancellor of Germany in the 1870's he observed that virtually all of his powerful enemies were men who were 65 years old or older. He persuaded the German legislature to pass legislation making 65 the mandatory age for retirement. It had nothing whatever to do with a decline in their mental faculties or a drop-off in productivity. For some strange reason other countries in Europe followed suit, and the policy was eventually adopted in America.

What an absolute tragedy to encourage people to quit when they are at the very peak of their intellect, wisdom, and experience! Could that be the reason that the only time the Bible mentions retirement it is as a punishment?

There's harmony and inner peace to be found in following a moral compass that points in the same direction, regardless of fashion or trend.

— Ted Koppel

For twenty-three years, Katherine Power was a fugitive. She had driven the getaway car in a bank robbery that ended in the death of a policeman. Extreme depression and the realization that she could not, would not, get better without taking responsibility for her part in the heinous crime led her to surrender.

Physically, she surrendered to the FBI; emotionally, she surrendered to survive. The self-imposed prison she had been living in was much worse than the physical building she would ultimately occupy.

Serenity, relief, and hope etched Katherine Power's face when the judge handed down her sentence of eight to twelve years. She was smiling the smile of someone who has been set free after years of unfathomable torture and solitary confinement. Confession is good for the soul.

Outstanding people have one thing in common: an absolute sense of mission.

If we had to drive from Dallas to Boston with no directions, maps, or signs, we would have a degree of fear. With directions, good maps, and clear road signs, that fear would largely disappear. Actually, very few of us would attempt that trip without directions and maps. Unfortunately, very few people are equipped with specific directions of how to navigate the highways of life. No wonder the overwhelming majority of people end up at the end of life's journey with just a fraction of what life has to offer.

Dr. Karl A. Menninger said, "Fears are educated into us and can, if we wish, be educated out." James Allen stated, "He who has conquered doubt and fear has conquered failure."

No one can make you feel inferior without your consent.

— Eleanor Roosevelt

Years ago, I read that a Rembrandt painting had sold for over one million dollars. As I read, I thought to myself, "What in the world would make some paint on a canvas worth so much money?" Then a couple of thoughts occurred to me. First, this was obviously a unique painting. Its rarity gave it value. Second, Rembrandt was a genius.

Then I started thinking about you. There are several billion people on earth today, but you are a rare, exclusive, different and unique being on the face of this earth. These qualities give you enormous value. The same God who created Rembrandt created you, and you are as precious in God's sight as Rembrandt or anyone else.

Confrontation doesn't always bring a solution to the problem, but until you confront the problem, there will be no solution.

— James Baldwin

There's strength in admitting a weakness. Most of us are vulnerable in certain areas of our lives, and those who are wise and ambitious will admit their weaknesses and vulnerability.

For example, I have a friend who became addicted to pornography and has broken the habit. Recognizing that weakness, he is careful not to have even the slightest exposure to anything of a pornographic nature. If he's in a place where the television set is on and there's suggestive language or behavior that is of a lustful or seductive nature, he immediately leaves the scene. That's smart.

If you have a weakness, be strong enough to admit it and get some help in whatever area that might be.

Today be aware of how you are spending your 1,440 beautiful moments, and spend them wisely.

You will never realize more than a small fraction of your potential as a wandering generality. You must become a meaningful specific. Unfortunately, most people have only a vague idea of what they want, and very few people consistently act on vague ideas. The typical person goes to work every day because that's what he did yesterday. If that's the only reason for going to work today, the odds are long that he will be no more effective today than he was yesterday.

Harry Emerson Fosdick said it best: "No steam or gas ever drives anything until it is confined. No Niagara is ever turned into light and power until it is tunneled. No life ever grows until it is focused, dedicated, disciplined."

Denial is not a river in Egypt; denial is ignoring the obvious.

I'm absolutely convinced that most people kid themselves when they say, "This member of the opposite sex and I are 'just' friends." That might well be true in the beginning of some relationships. But in far too many cases, this "friendship" with the opposite sex, over a period of time because of mutual respect for the intellect or professional capabilities of the other, changes into something more than friendship.

Tragically, most attractions are denied in the beginning with catastrophic results. When this happens, rather than pretend that it didn't happen: (a) honestly acknowledge what has happened; (b) remember your commitment to your mate; and (c) remind yourself of the proven fact that there are no "harmless" flirtations.

When obstacles arise, change your direction to reach your goal, not the decision to get there.

Once when I took a flight from Los Angeles to Dallas, our scheduled departure was for 5:15 PM, but due to unavoidable delays we didn't leave until 6:03 PM. When we left the Los Angeles airport, we headed for Dallas, but within 20 minutes the situation had changed. The crosswinds were slightly different from those predicted before takeoff, so we were slightly off course. The captain made a slight adjustment and we were again headed for Dallas. My point is this: when we were a little off our course, the captain didn't turn the plane around and return to Los Angeles to make a fresh start.

Even so, as you head toward your goals, be prepared to make some slight adjustments in your course.

Your mind acts on what you feed it.

It's like the story of the woman who had a serious kidney infection. An operation was scheduled to remove one of her kidneys. After they put her to sleep, they ran the final test, and discovered that the operation was not necessary. They didn't remove the kidney, but when she awoke, the first thing she said was, "Oh, my back. Oh, I hurt. Oh, I feel so bad. Oh, it hurts." When she was told they had not performed the operation, she was slightly embarrassed. Obviously, she went to sleep expecting to wake up hurting, and that is exactly what she did! In her mind, her pains were just as real as if the operation had been performed.

Your mind doesn't know the difference between reality and fantasy. Feed it good thoughts.

Education and intelligence are not the same thing.

Three of the most intelligent and successful people I know finished the 3rd, 5th, and 8th grades. Henry Ford quit school at 14 and Thomas J. Watson, founder of IBM, went from a $6.00/week salesman to Chairman of the Board. A limited "formal" education is no excuse and certainly no reason to have a poor self-image. Obviously education is important, but dedication is even more important. Get rid of your excuses for failure, find reasons and methods to succeed, and dedicate yourself to utilizing the potential you possess and your education, or lack thereof, will not even be an issue.

Unfortunately, many "educated" people never succeed in life because they are not "motivated" to put their imagination to work to utilize their knowledge. That's one less excuse!

The most destitute person in the world is the one without a smile.

Join the smile and compliment club. When you smile at someone and they smile back, you automatically feel better even if they don't smile back. You immediately become richer by giving that person your smile. Ditto for the compliment. When you sincerely compliment a person or extend him a courtesy he is going to receive a direct benefit and like himself better. It is impossible for you to make someone feel better and not feel better yourself.

One of the best ways to make anyone else feel better is to spread optimism and good cheer. I'm convinced that everyone, including you, just naturally feels better when exposed to a cheerful, optimistic individual almost regardless of the nature or length of the contact. So, smile — with your face and with your heart.

The chains of habit are too weak to be felt until they are too strong to be broken.

This is evidenced by the number of people who have nicotine "fits" from the time they run out of cigarettes until they can buy, beg, borrow, or steal another. I've seen an otherwise healthy 200-pound man reduced to a quivering mass by a craving for a cigarette that weighed less than 1/10th of an ounce. It almost makes me wish we were creatures of logic instead of creatures of emotion.

Yes, habits are funny things. What's funny, or rather tragic, is that bad habits are so predictable and avoidable. Despite this, there are people by the millions who insist on acquiring habits that are bad, expensive, and create problems. The habit they weren't going to get, got them.

Choose good habits and the bad ones can't sneak up on you.

If you learn from a defeat, you haven't really lost.

My friend, Cavett Robert, takes a philosophical, refreshing and common-sense approach to a journey into Negativeville as he observes, "Nobody fails by falling down or getting despondent. They only fail if they stay down or negative." Cavett stresses that you should be like a leaky tire. A defeat should take something out of you and deflate you a bit. If it didn't, it would be a strong indication you not only didn't mind losing, but you weren't emotionally involved in wanting to win.

I'm talking about your internal reaction to defeat. Obviously, I don't feel you should pout or throw a tantrum. Be gracious and mature and the chances are good you will enter the winner's circle after the next encounter.

Go as far as you can see, and when you get there you will always be able to see farther.

Without long-range goals, you are likely to be overcome by short-range frustrations. The reason is simple. Everybody is not as interested in your success as you are. You might occasionally feel that some people are standing in the way and deliberately slowing your progress, but in reality the biggest person standing in your way is you.

Occasionally, circumstances arise that are beyond your control. If you don't have long-range goals, then temporary obstacles can be needlessly frustrating. A setback can be a stepping-stone and not a stumbling block. When you have that long-range goal it's easier.

If you wait until all the lights are "green" before you leave home, you'll never get started on your trip to the top.

Success occurs when opportunity meets preparation.

Many times it is just over the hill or around the corner. Sometimes it takes that extra push to climb that hill or round that curve. The wit was right when he said, "If you have enough push you don't have to worry about pull."

President Calvin Coolidge wrote, "Nothing in the world can take the place of persistence. Talent will not. Nothing is more common than unsuccessful men with talent. Genius will not. Unrewarded genius is almost a proverb. Education will not. The world is full of educated derelicts. Persistence, determination, and hard work make the difference."

Wouldn't it be wonderful if our mind growled like our stomach does when it is hungry?

From the neck down, very few people are worth more than $100.00 a week. From the neck up, there is no limit to what an individual is worth. So what do we do? We feed our stomachs, the $100.00 part below our necks, every day. How often do we feed our minds, the part that has no limit to its value, earning and happiness potential? Most of us feed it accidentally and occasionally, if it's convenient. The excuse we often give is our lack of time. This is ridiculous. If you have "time" to feed the $100.00 part of you every day, doesn't it make sense you should take time to feed the part which has no ceiling to its potential?

Happiness is like a kiss. In order to get any good out of it, you have to give it to someone else.

Many people honestly believe they will be happy when they get into a home of their own; they will be happy when they get all of the little things that frequently convert a house into a home — but they won't. Then they'll be happy when they get the mortgage paid — but they won't. Then they will be happy when they get their second home down at the lake or up on the mountainside — but they won't.

The reason is simple: It makes no difference where you go, there you are. And it makes no difference what you have, there's always more to want. Until you are happy with who you are, you will never be happy because of what you have.

You are at the top when...

1. You've made friends with the past, are focused on the present, and optimistic about your future.

2. You have made friends of your adversaries and have gained the love and respect of those who know you best.

3. You are filled with faith, hope, and love and live without anger, greed, guilt, envy, or thoughts of revenge.

4. You know that failure to stand for what is morally right is the prelude to being the victim of what is criminally wrong.

5. You are mature enough to delay gratification and shift your focus from your rights to your responsibilities.

6. You love the unlovable and give hope to the hopeless, friendship to the friendless, and encouragement to the discouraged.

7. You know that success doesn't make you, and failure doesn't break you.

8. You are at peace with God and man.

9. You clearly understand that failure is an event, not a person; that yesterday ended last night, and today is your brand-new day.

10. You know that "he who would be the greatest among you must become the servant of all."

11. You are pleasant to the grouch, courteous to the rude, and generous to the needy because you know the long-term benefits of receiving.

12. You recognize, confess, develop, and use your God given physical, mental, and spiritual abilities to the glory of God and for the benefit of mankind.

13. You stand in front of the Creator of the universe, and He says to you, "Well done, thou good and faithful servant."

About the Author

Zig Ziglar, one of the most popular communicators of his day, is known as the "Motivators' Motivator." More than three million people have attended Zig's live presentations, and millions of others have been inspired by his training apes and videos. A prolific author, Zig's books have sold more than four million copies worldwide, and his syndicated column, Zig Ziglar's Encouraging Word, now appears in newspapers nationwide. His long list of awards includes, "Communicator of the Year," by the Sales and Marketing Executives International. But what makes Zig most proud is being happily married to his wife of 49 years, Jean, whom he lovingly calls "Sugar Baby."

For additional information on seminars, scheduling speaking engagements, or to write the author, please address your correspondence to:

Zig Ziglar
3330 Earhart, Suite 204
Carrollton, TX 75006-5026

Additional copies of this book are available from your local bookstore.

Tulsa, Oklahoma